PATH OF
THE MAGUS

Magus Zeta

Print Edition
Path of the Magus
Copyright © 2015 J D Lovil.
ALL RIGHTS RESERVED

ASIN: 9781520237008
Independently Published

Disclaimer

This book is intended to be a source of information for the beginner in the Art of Magick, to understand the path that they are preparing to walk. The Reader may always be the singular exception in the Magickal path that they experience. If that is the case, it should feed their sense of superiority, as they watch their fellow Novices and Adepts on the Path struggling with the realities of Magick.

.

1 Why Pursue Magick?

THERE ARE FOUR MAJOR forms of inquiry into the nature of existence, with a subgenre of inquiry that spans the other four. The subgenre is Philosophy, with the four forms being those of Science, Religion, Spiritualism, and Magick. Each of these forms makes assumptions about the nature of reality unique to their form, and each attempts to answer the question of existence from a different angle to the others.

The form of Science tries to answer the question of how the universe works. This involves breaking down events and properties into their component parts, just as you would break down an internal combustion engine into its components in order to find and fix the offending part. We conduct science with an objective of finding useful ways to manipulate our world with new information about how the universe works.

The form of Religion tries to answer the question of who made the universe and attempts to secure the benefits of knowing this by worship or other appropriate actions, which will appease the deity or deities, and get them to help secure benefits for us. On a practical level, it is a great system for securing social and political power in the hands of the religious leaders.

The form of Spiritualism is a bit more nebulous. It seeks out the existence of non-physical entities such as ghosts, specters, spirits, the semi-physical entities such as the Sidhe, the ancient spirits of places, elementals in all their forms. Spiritualism even broaches the areas of religious entities such as angels, demons and the ancient pagan gods and entities. In the Spiritualist School of thought, these entities are seen as spiritual rather than religious or physical beings. Most forms of Paganism belongs to this category of form.

Each of these forms has their appended practices. Religion has Satanism, Atheism, Satanic or demon based witchcraft. Science has a spectrum of viewpoints, from a purely mechanical and physical view of the universe to a view of the cosmos as containing a universal mind which cannot be distinguished from the creator God himself. Spiritualism has Shamanism, and Voodoo (in its various forms), and hundreds of forms of spiritualism that exists are corrupted by bits and pieces of science, religion, and Magick was thrown into the mix.

Magick is attached to all of these appended practices since it partakes of all of the other forms in some of its practices. Magick in its purest form is an offshoot of the scientific process, seeking to make sense of existence by examining the universe, and seeking to gain benefits both exotic and mundane from the knowledge. Pure Magick is what we will consider in this book.

Of all the disciplines, Science and Magick are the ones most closely resembling each other. Each of them examines the universe around them and attempts to discover ways to manipulate reality in a way that is beneficial to the beings involved.

Science examines and explores the components of the system and then tries to build tools to make life easier or more interesting. Magick examines the system as a whole and seeks to find patterns within it that will yield useful means of manipulating the world around the practitioner or to secure useful information for him.

I am using the definition of a system that is used by both disciplines. In this situation, a system is the set of things that are connected to each other to create a whole. The context for the system connection may vary with the situation, of course. The planet Earth is a system that maintains a biosphere. The Solar System is a system that maintains the Earth and other planets in solar orbit. The galaxy is a system, which contains and maintains the Solar System in a community of stars. You get the idea.

Ancient Science, Religion, Spiritualism, and Magick were different aspects of the same discipline. The Wise, or Magi, in the far distant past, watched the world around them and made observations of the heavens, the plants, and all of the various necessary activities of tribal life to seek useful information to help their people thrive.

One of the first things that the Magi learned is that the world seemed to be influenced by the needs, thoughts, and actions of the people in it. There have always been those who can see some future events, or that can see things hidden by distance, secrecy, or some other barrier. People exhibit strange powers in unusual circumstances, which cannot be explained by a purely materialistic viewpoint.

Some of the useful talents that people the world over have exhibited are telepathy, precognition, astral projection and/or remote viewing, bilocation, and telekinesis. There are also those who seem to be able to talk to the dead, or to other spiritual beings, those who can curse or bless those around them, or that can create a spirit-like entity to do their wills, and those who have even stranger abilities.

Observations by the Magi led to the creation of astrology, astronomy, mathematics, alchemy and its descendent chemistry, Herbalism and its descendent pharmacology. It also led to the practice of meditation, acupressure, and acupuncture, and eventually to biofeedback techniques and other brain function techniques.

Each of the disciplines is dependent on the nature of the practitioner. Science and Magick require a mind that is somewhat introverted, and that questions the nature of the world in an appropriate way for the discipline to be a proper venue for their quest. In science, the practitioner must feel an overwhelming need to understand how the world works, and how its parts create the world that we see. Magick is more concerned with the meaning of the reality that the practitioner finds himself in, and is concerned with how the many parts of the world are related to the functioning of it.

Spiritualism is close to Magick in its orientation. It also seeks Meaning in reality, but it considers that meaning to be related to other entities, and to the relationships between them. This may seem to be similar to the orientation of Religion, but it is very different.

Religion involves the abrogation of one's responsibility for existence, and the transfer of that responsibility to a larger than life God or gods, who bear the brunt of the decisions that guide the life of the practitioner. The primary goal of Religion is to give away the power necessary for making life decisions to another Being and dispensing with the need for independent thought and choice in life.

The practice and results of Magick have been part of the human experience throughout history, but it was not until the formulation of Quantum Theory that a framework existed to use as a sort of Unified Magickal Theory. With the idea of the Observer based collapse of quantum states and the changes of the Worldline that this process involved, we now have some idea of how Magick actually works.

This book is based on the idea of Quantum Magicks and describes the sort of realization and life events that will take place in the practice and study of the subject. For the most part, the path of the practitioner in a Magickal school would be the same, regardless of the particular school that pertains. It is my belief that Quantum Magick holds the most answers for the Practitioner. Since we know which bowl contains the good candy, this book will concentrate on that Magickal School.

2 A Quantum Sorcery Brief

IN ORDER TO FAMILIARIZE the reader with the part that quantum theory plays in the performance of Magick, it is necessary to speak of the discoveries that led to quantum mechanics, as they are known today. This is not a study in science history so I will try not to speak of persons or dates of the various discoveries, although I am not responsible if a couple of those factoids creep into the story. Just consider it a sort of Tourette's syndrome.

The electron and other elementary particles were considered actual physical bits of matter about a hundred years ago. Science discovered that these particles occasionally acted like a wave instead of hard particles in certain situations. Other times, they appeared to act just as the old theories predicted. This resulted in much head-scratching and the frequent accusation of one or the other of the scientists conducting inferior science. Eventually, the majority of scientists reluctantly agreed that something unusual was taking place.

Experimental Scientists also established that certain properties of the observed particles **could not** be determined. If the observer noted the position of the particle, they would not be able to establish the speed and direction in which the particle was traveling. If they sought to restrain the particle in a potential well, such as by using a strong magnetic field to force the particle's path, they could not be certain that the particle would be in the position that theory and mathematics said that it would, when they looked.

By process of elimination, they determined that the properties of the particle were uncertain, and did not depend on any of the experimental system parameters. It was as if the particle was not really in any position until someone looked at it. The only consistent determinate of the particles circumstances seemed to be the Observer.

An experimental procedure called **The Double Slit Experiment** compounded the mystery of the subatomic particle's true behavior. In this experiment, the Experimenters emitted an electron toward a metal barrier with two small slits in the metal and a photographic plate behind to barrier to document through which one of the slits the electron passed. The experiment led to a troubling conclusion. Sometimes the electron acted like the hard particle it was considered to be historically, and the electron would go through one of the slits, creating a single impact photograph of the event.

Sometimes the electron would be recorded as going through both of the slits, and the photograph would show impact and interference patterns, indicating that the electron acted as though it was in both positions, and was acting as a wave as well. Subsequent experiments with more slits produced still more complex interference patterns, and more indications that the electron went through all of the slits.

The only thing that seemed to change the results of the experiment was if there is an observer watching as the experiment completes. Every time that an Observer watched, as the experiment concluded, the photographic plates would show an obvious discrete path for a particle through one, and only one, of the slits. When no Observer was present, the photographic plates would show an interference pattern, such as what one would expect if a wave traveled through both of the slits.

Recently, the experimental results have gotten even stranger. A French team recently replaced the slits with an interferometer, and introduced randomly beam splitters, which would obscure the path of the electron, but was a random event. Each time the splitter was present, the path was unobservable to the detector, and the electron exhibited the interference pattern that is so mysterious. When it was not present, the electron would act as a solid particle.

The strange thing is that nobody knew in advance which of the experimental runs would be observable, and which would not, until *after* the completed run. The only way to explain this result is to assume that *observation determined in the future could affect the outcome of the present experiment.*

People have tried to discount this result with many erroneous arguments. They say that it is a result of actual physical interference with the particles due to the observation process, even though this does not explain the wave versus particle paradox. They say that this is not an observer effect, merely the result of the uncertainty principle. There is definitely a connection between the uncertainty principle and the observer effect, but when the Observer has a direct effect on the type of resultant outcome regardless of methods of observation, that argument seems to be a bit off.

If you conduct the experiment with ten slits instead of two or three, you get an interference pattern that reflects the probability of the particle going through each slit measured as the intensity of the interference effect. If an Observer is present, you get one impact record through one of the slits only. How do we explain that?

Every system that exists has a quantum state, which defines all of the parts of the system. Every particle has a quantum state equation. Every atom has a quantum state equation. Every molecule, every world, star system or galaxy has a quantum state equation. The universe defines itself by its own unique quantum state equation.

When no Observer is present during the ten slit experiment, you get the interference pattern that indicates that each of the ten possible outcomes all exists in our world until the Observer is present, at which time all but one of the outcomes disappear from our world.

Nobody knows why the Observer has such a strange effect on the event, effectively collapsing the quantum states for the particle to only one outcome. Nobody knows where the other nine possible outcomes go to for sure, but logic suggests an answer to both questions.

There is another theory out there that has a bearing on this experimental result. This theory states that all possible outcomes of all events are preserved by the branching of the world line at that point. That would mean in a ten-outcome event, nine new Worldlines would be created, and the Observer would only be able to see the one that still manifested itself in the Observer's universe.

In this MANY WORLDS THEORY, parallel universes branch off from ours like branches of a tree with every event that has more than one possible outcome. That means that this universe breeds an infinite number of possible near clone universes, and each of them continues to grow branch universes of their own.

We see evidence of these other universes in many ways. We see evidence of all of the outcomes existing in our universe until they go away. We also have personal experiences that support the idea of other universes, and we can access them to some degree.

A question comes out of the many slit experiment. Why do our results seem to be that the particles act like waves when unobserved, but they act like particles when observed? I think I have an obvious answer.

We are trained from grade school to think of electrons and other 'elementary particles' as solid little objects, not waves. Since we expect the experiment to yield evidence that supports our unconscious picture of what a particle is, somehow our *expectation* causes the particle to manifest *as a particle* when observed.

This same set of unconscious expectations about how the world around us works and looks seem to act upon the world around us to produce the expected events and results. You can see this in people's positive or negative expectations of the events of their day. The same person that was expecting trouble yesterday, and received it, may have good expectations for today and will receive them also.

One of the things that are obvious to everyone is that a person's attitude toward life has a real effect on their lives. Persons with a positive attitude generally have positive results, and the negative people get negative results. These people believe that they will get a certain sort of outcome, and they expect that outcome. The extent to which people receive the results in life that they expect to get is so great that any statistical treatment of the results as a random process would return insane conclusions.

At this point, one has to get into more subjective opinions about what is happening in these phenomena. I believe that all of these parallel universes are cospatial. They overlay the same coordinates in space-time that exists in our universe. We are not easily able to visualize this conservative idea of parallel universes.

Imagine, if you will, that the eyes of the Observer connect **all** of these universes. The Observer chooses to see the universe that he expects, but he is also able to see all of the other parallel universes at will. All he has to do is to change his expectations of what he will see, and the universes that correspond to those expectations will be visible to him.

Let us review what we have learned so far. Our take on quantum mechanics and using the Many Worlds Theory, is that all events have multiple outcomes. All but one of these outcomes vanishes from our universe when the Observer resolves the quantum state by seeing the event, and the resolution appears always to be in line with the expectations of the Observer.

The Observer resolves the quantum state of everything around him on a continual basis. There is never a time when the Observer is not actively affecting the world around him. The unconscious or Undermind works continuously to bring the expectations of the Observer into reality.

There are two ways to interpret the idea of parallel universes. You may consider them to be discrete universes laid out in space-time in a breath's variance with our world. You may also consider them actually to be a part of our universe itself, and the space-time that we live in is a Chaotic Plenum, infinitely filled with all possible event outcomes from all points, the past, present, and future of our universe.

Either way you look at it, our Underminds are supreme Sorcerers, capable of resolving the world about us to fit exactly our expectations of it. For most of us, the process of resolving the quantum states is unconscious Magick, produced by that part of our mind that has nearly infinite power, but no ambition or care for our health and happiness. We are all Quantum Sorcerers, but most of us are sleeping Sorcerers.

Everyone creates the world around him or her all of the time, but most of us have no idea of how to take conscious control of this ability. Quantum Sorcery is the training manual for how to take that power and use it consciously to better our worlds.

The pursuit of true Magick is a lifelong endeavor. This book is written so that you are familiar with the stages of that journey of discovery, and so that you understand that you are making progress when the going seems to get too hard. Read on, think about the process with an open mind, and you will become the Magus!

3 A Deeper History

MODERN HISTORIANS LOVE to put their biased spin on the history of our fair planet, and on the history of our species. They will insist that they are right, even if the story they spin is a pale shadow of the true history of our planet and our species. It is important to understand our origins to understand what we can do.

About 4.75 billion years ago, our sun was nothing more than a large cloud of mostly Hydrogen, with a smattering of Helium and traces of other elements in the mix. It was slowly collapsing into a spherical mass of gasses, and it would have eventually have become sufficiently compressed by gravity to begin the process of fusion. It had some help.

Somewhere within two light years of the gas cloud, a large red giant star began the collapse that would result in a supernova. In the last few seconds of the supernova event, the star produced large quantities of heavy elements, which the resulting explosion expelled from the system behind a massive radiation emission, all headed toward the cloud of gas that would become our sun.

The radiation made it to our system first, passing through the system in a tidal wave of energies, which acted like a hand pressing on the side of the cloud balloon, forcing accelerated compression of the cloud, and Hydrogen fusion began. Shortly after, the cloud of heavy elements entered the system of the newly form star Sol and began a complex and chaotic orbit of the new star.

Within a few million years of the formation of the sun, the masses of heavy elements from the former red giant star had in large part compressed into planetary bodies of varying sizes. Orbiting bodies crowded the system, and they frequently collided with each other. The process of creation and destruction of planetary bodies was ferocious and unrelenting.

The planet, which would one day become Earth, was a rocky island in the sky, with a surface still partially molten due to the heat of its collapse into a spherical body. It was a forbidding place, with a bit of atmosphere of toxic gasses, which were the product of degassing of the molten rock. This was no place for life to live!

Around about 200 million years after the sun began fusion, the Earth circled the sun in its lonely orbit, with only the occasional mass that collided with the planet to keep it company. The heavens were full of comets and planets, asteroids and dust. One day, a large planet passed very close to the young Earth.

Planets keep their mass with them using the power of gravitation. Every other body in the universe also pulls at a planet's mass, but usually, they exert far too weak a pull to drag any mass away from the planet. When another body comes close enough, it can pull mass into space toward it, if it exerts the same or stronger gravitational pull as the planet.

The traveler planet passed by the Earth at a distance of about 11,000 miles, just short of the Roche Limit at which the bodies would tear themselves completely apart. Even so, a geyser of crustal material from both planets made it into the space between the two bodies before the traveler continued on its way. This material slowly collapsed together into the body now known as our moon.

About 3.9 billion years ago, life first appeared on Earth from a combination of panspermia and biochemistry. The first form of life was anaerobic, simple and single-celled, and it mutated rapidly with the early Earth's biochemistry available to it.

About 100 million years after life had established itself on Earth, a large multi-form species of star travelers, comfortable in the anaerobic atmosphere, came to Earth to stay. And stay they did, for the next one-half billion years, until the coming of the next great cataclysm. This disaster was a series of three large planetoid-sized asteroids that struck the earth in an interval of 50 million years, which nearly wiped the Earth clean of life about 3.3 billion years ago.

It took life on Earth millions of years to recover, and the great designs and structures of the Star Travelers were cast down. They left the planet shortly after the strikes to find quieter homes. The Earth continued to host life and an anaerobic atmosphere for nearly another billion years. Around 3 billion years ago, the first oxygen-producing life evolved, but the oxygen was sequestered by the iron content in the environment before it could significantly alter the atmosphere.

About 2.5 billion years ago, a new form of life called cyanobacteria developed, and oxygen-producing life was here on Earth to stay. By 2.3 billion years ago, there was sufficient oxygen in the atmosphere to begin killing off the anaerobic bacterial life. This also ushered in a new 'Snowball Earth' glaciation called the **Huronian glaciation,** which lasted for about 300 million years, and ended about 2.1 billion years ago.

About 700 million years ago, the oxygenation of the atmosphere and the fertile seabeds conspired to create the first of the multicellular creatures, the Ediacarans. Within the first million years, multiple evolutionary branches of this asymmetric form of life exploded into existence, and one branch developed size and intelligence, and for a few million years enjoyed the status of masters of the planet. For unknown reasons, they left Earth and sought something among the stars for which we have no concept.

Life continued here on our planet, with the occasional visitor, and more than a few of these visitors meddled with the life forms they found here. None of them stayed long by geological standards. The most persistent visitors were the ones who were related to the life they found here. The ones who began tinkering with the proto-primates about 35 million years ago had many genes in common with our primate and then hominid species, and they had come from a place that made this Earth seem like a planet from the distant past.

The first ones to tinker with the genetics of Man were inhabitants of a distant shadow, where the evolution of a Homo sapiens variant had occurred millions of years earlier than here so that the visitors were even more divergent from our species than the Greys that are seen today. The visitors, which we can call the Archons, were the result of a self-directed evolution involving Nanotech, cybernetic implants, and borrowing from alien life forms during their multi-million-year exploration of their space. They manipulated the genetics of a Lemur style primate to create the first of the ape variety of primates, looking somewhat like a very primitive chimpanzee.

Other aliens interfered with the natural course of evolution of our branch of the animal kingdom over the next few million years, usually by changing geographic locations of the ancestral forms, and by facilitating breeding programs when needed. It was not until the advent of the human variant known by some as the Anunnaki that a concerted effort was made to modify the species.

Between four and five million years ago, the first group of Anunnaki arrived here on earth from a close shadow Earth, and they immediately established kingdoms, complete with palace politics, rivalries, and competitions between the 'gods.' They were dissatisfied with a world without subjects to rule, and so they used advanced genetic knowledge to create several varieties of primitive hominid forms, including several varieties of Homo erectus, including Homo habilis, Homo Egaster and other early members of the genus Homo.

They took a few risks in their manipulations, at one point, creating the six-fingered red-haired giants, which are known throughout the world as man-eating hunters of man. After realizing that the Giants were not suitable subjects, the Anunnaki terminated that experiment, but not before a few specimens escaped to the wild and then spread all over the world.

Saving some of the knowledge gained in that failed experiment, the Anunnaki developed the first variant of the species we now know as the Neanderthal, a more peaceful, smaller and more human-like version of the red-haired giants. The gods were content with these creatures for a short time, but soon, they came to look upon the Neanderthal more as pets than as subjects and were dissatisfied with the idea of them as their subjects.

Finally, the Anunnaki created the Cro-Magnon form of humanity, which was essentially an ultra-healthy seven-foot tall form of Modern Man, and which looked like a slightly smaller form of the Anunnaki themselves. Finally, the gods had the subjects they needed to make their kingdoms feel like true realms. This was about two million years ago, some 1.8 million years before modern science thinks that it happened.

Over the period between then and now, the Anunnaki expanded their realm throughout the world, establishing kingdoms, basically wherever a Pyramid or a Ziggurat can be found. They established the ancient towns and countries of the Indus Valley, Sumer, Egypt, Atlantis, and several other almost unknown ancient civilizations.

Being few in number, the Anunnaki delegated many authorities to their human subjects, and they interbred with them as well. By the time that we know as the period of ancient Sumer, which was the second incarnation of that Empire, almost all of the Anunnaki had blended totally into the genetic mix of humanity, with only a few of the most ancient of them still extant as evidence of the existence of the gods.

This brings us to the present day. Humanity is a blend of the genus Homo and Anunnaki genes and is the sole remaining source of Anunnaki genes in the world today. Many of our ancient people had advanced to spaceflight, colonized other planets and fallen back to primitive circumstances.

No matter if we find our way to parallel universes or other star systems, we will find that our kin has already been there. In this region of our universe, we are not alone. We will find our relatives everywhere.

4 The Initiate

INITIATES TO THE MYSTERIES of an Occult School of Magick encounter a very new way of life, with every aspect of it changed and unsettling. They have to learn to look at the world around them with new eyes, and they will spend much of their time developing the magical tools that they will be using to practice Magick.

To practice Magick, no matter what form of Magick practiced, the Initiate will have to conceptualize the Mind Palace or the Sanctum in which they will practice the Occult arts. They must also create the Magical Persona, or the person that they are when practicing the Arts. The Student will have to rethink every expectation, belief, and opinion, which the Student holds, that has been in any way is related to the Reality in which they live.

The hardest task of the Initiate is to accept that the universe around them is truly subject to modification by the actions of the Sorcerer. We all are subject to conditioning by our culture that ingrains an unconscious belief that the world around us is a hard and concrete place that is **what it is**. We find it hard to refuse this erroneous belief, even after life gives us endless examples of the results of our mental processes upon the world around us.

Beyond belief in the Magick that the initiate will be practicing, he will also need to develop the place and personality for the Magickal practice. First, he will need to understand and *feel* the magical nature of the world on an experiential level. There is nothing like seeing to believe, and there is nothing like feeling to accept the forces from within and without, with which the initiate will learn to work.

The Initiate is essentially a Freshman Student in the subject. If his subject studies had a specific course name, they would all be followed by the course number 101. The first lessons that He must learn are that his beliefs and his expectations rule the outcome of every aspect of his life. He is far more in control of his destiny than he ever suspected. His mind will bring him whatever he expects throughout his life, so prevalently so that he will be intimidated by the responsibility.

The first lesson the Initiate must master is the one that teaches him that the world he lives in is a place of Magick. The second lesson is to learn a proper meditative process, one that will meld together the arts of calmness, hypnosis, visualization and dreaming into a seamless whole.

Once he has achieved noticeable results in the realm of meditation, the Initiate must envision the Magickal Persona that he will be in the performance of the Art. The appearance, behavior, and movements of this Persona must be a distillation of creative power to the mind of the Initiate. The purpose of the Persona is to convince the Greater Mind, the Undermind that lives below the conscious one, that the Persona is the real Initiate, and that He is indeed capable of commanding the forces with which he will be working.

Once the Initiate has begun to work with the Persona, he will discover that he has been creating and using similar Personas all of his life, personalities better suited to accomplishing the tasks at hand than is his own innate personality. At some point, he will reach an Epiphany, where he realizes that even his innate personality is simply a Persona that he has constructed and put on at an early age, to deal with the outer world.

This realization of the 'Thinness' of the personality will lead inexorably to the discovery that the personality is but a thin layer of clothing on the true mind that dwells within him. He will discover that his true mind is much greater than he has ever thought. It is capable of miracles, but it has few desires or ambitions. It is conscious, but its identity is of that sort that one wears within a dream, more a point of view than a creation of the memory and Back-story of the creature that bears the name of the Initiate and dwells entirely within the sunlit world.

The Undermind *is a dreaming mind*, and the dream it dreams is the reality that surrounds the Initiate. It is a mind that experiences that reality and moves within it as in a dream. When this becomes known to the Initiate, he is ready to consider the nuances of that Truth.

One of the techniques that the Initiate will learn is the visualizing of his life as a movie on the screen of his mind. At some point, as he practices this, he will realize an important truth. He will have begun the training, hoping to obtain those things in life that he has desired, by the use of Magick. During his session of visualization, he will discover that the Undermind is a Jinn that grants his expectations of life, not his desires. Indeed, almost every expectation that he has ever had of life is faithfully granted to him, both positive and negative.

The driving force of the Initiate is **Desire**, the desire of those things that he considers to be of value that he lacks in life. He will realize the paradox that he must overcome with his Persona is to turn those things, which he expects of Life, into the things that he desires of Life.

This realization will lead him to understand that two things determine his expectations, those being memory and beliefs. Visualization can be the tool that counters the memories that create expectation. The Undermind cannot distinguish between a detailed visualization and a 'real' event; hence, the Initiate can manufacture memories of receiving his desires via visualization, enhancing the expectation of those desires delivered for the Undermind on which to act.

Beliefs are at the core of the Persona that the Initiate will construct, and the person can choose to believe. The Initiate can choose to believe in God, or gods, he must choose to believe in magick, if he wishes to engage in it. A Belief is essentially a shortcut to the expectations that one has, and it is, in large part, under the control of the thin conscious mind to create.

Therefore, the Initiate will carefully envision and create the Magickal Persona to give the Undermind the expectations of life that the Initiate wishes to possess, knowing that the Undermind will faithfully deliver the expected results to him. The more detailed he makes his Persona; the better will be his results.

Finally, the Initiate will construct his Mind Palace, or his imagined Sanctum, which he will see as the location where he conducts his acts of Sorcery and Magick. This castle of the mind should be spacious, and it should hold within its boundaries doors that will act as portals, a place of rest and one of meditation, a place where great forces can be summoned and banished in solitude.

For some, this will manifest as a cave, or perhaps it will be an open space such as a Stonehenge analog. For some, it is an actual castle, and for others, it possesses only an interior of endless rooms and spaces, with no exterior ever seen. It may even be a forest bower or a place where lay-lines intersect. Whatever it is, it should be a place of mental security and liberation for the Initiate, for he will cast his Art within its boundaries.

A part of the Mind Palace is an Entity, which is its protector, and the familiar or ally of the Initiate. The Initiate will envision and create it, and task it with whatever he wishes it to do. Usually, the Protector is in an animal form, but there are no limitations on the form it must take.

The Protector of the Mind Palace is a Tulpa, an artificial Elemental created by the mind of the Initiate. The most common form used is that of a dog, or another canine, as they already occupy that niche in our exterior world of protector and companion. A Tulpa is a 'mind form,' and the name comes from the Tibetan practice of creating them.

The Initiate will be occupied learning about and creating his tools, using the techniques of meditation, visualization, and self-hypnosis. He will create his Magickal Persona, Mind Palace, and Protector, and will learn to understand the world as a place where his Magicks can have an effect. Once he has mastered these lessons and created these tools, he will be ready to become the Novice.

5 The Novice

NOVICES TO THE MYSTERIES of an Occult School of Magick have learned of the structures that they will use in their Magickal actions. They are familiar with the procedures and viewpoints required of them to practice their craft, and of the Magickal nature of the universe that they live in. They have built the magical tools that they will use to practice Magick, and they are slowly becoming better and better in their use.

The Novice meditates daily, using visualization to alter the personal history that the Undermind sees, and by this process, giving the Undermind new instructions on what to bring to him or her.

The Novice holds the image of his Mind Palace and his Magickal Persona in his mind's eye, but he will not have perfect control over these visualizations at first. He meditates daily, and he practices the alteration of the world around him, but his meditations are subject to the occasional interference, and more often than not, he cannot see the clear results of his magical workings.

He is slowly coming to accept that the universe is much more susceptible to the Sorcerer's workings than the average person believes, but he is still attempting to overcome the conditioning that we all grow up with against that concept. Part of the time, he lives as though the world around him is truly the malleable place that his lessons have taught him it is, but most of the time, he slips back into the mundane 'world as a concrete reality' conditioning that he believed in, before his practice of the Art.

The Novice will continue to practice the Art, through times of frustration, and doubt, and times when he begins to believe that he has been deluding himself all along. He will practice, and slowly but surely, he will begin to see the changes that he makes in the world, and he will occasionally *feel* the Magicks in the world.

The Novice is practicing the craft, but he seldom sees a clear effect of his practice. His job is to use the techniques that he has learned, and, slowly but surely, overcome his doubts in the matter of Magicks. This lesson, as are all the **important** lessons, is a matter of three steps forward, two steps back. He will advance in his Art if he persists. There are many who fail at this step.

The motivation of the Novice is to gain power over his world. He has yet to understand that Knowledge is more important than power, and Wisdom is most important of all. The Power that the Novice seeks is without the completeness that Knowledge brings, and without the balance, that Wisdom brings.

The dreaming mind continues to dream, and the dream of the mind slowly becomes a part of the reality that the Novice finds, but his advances are glacially slow, and he does not always see the progress he makes. His visualizations of the Mind Palace and his own Persona are becoming much more concrete, but he still sometimes finds that odd alterations take place within the visions, and he has not yet gained the understanding of which to heed, and which to set aside.

The Novice has not yet found the way to set his Identity aside. The Undermind does not process its identity recursively; that is the tenacious instinct of the Conscious mind. When one goes about the task of working Magick, the Identity of the worker is only useful in the creation of goals. It is through the expectations of the Undermind that the Magicks work. Once the ego has established these expectations, it is time to get out of the way of the Undermind and let it do the work. When the worker dons the garment of the Persona, he is wearing a skin of tools, not necessarily a skin of Identity.

The Novice does not understand this. He thinks that when he becomes his Magickal Persona, he has changed the person that he is, but he thinks that he is still ego driven. The Persona is a focus, not a person. When you work Magicks, the closer you are to the Undermind, the better the Magick works. For the duration of the working, one must give up the desires, needs, and obsessions of the person, and just **Be**.

The biggest problem the Novice faces is this persistent, need to use his conscious mind, to see the world about him. The urge to gain power, the need to impress, and to acquire things and opportunities are all ego driven, and the Novice has all of these urges and needs thundering through his head. When he can clear himself of these things, he will be ready to enter the world of the Adept.

6 The Adept

THE ADEPT TO THE MYSTERIES of an Occult School of Magick has found many foci for their Magickal activities. They have been conditioned by constant repetition to expect a 'supernatural' result from their practice of meditation, visualization and other means of intention that they employ. They have come to see themselves as the Persona that they put on to accomplish their intended tasks.

The Novice had the problem of shedding his personality to practice Magicks. This was a problem, primarily because he began his study of the Art to fulfill his identity-centric goals. The question he had to answer was this one. How do you fulfill your desires, which originate in the ego-driven part of the mind, and divest yourself of that ego identity at the same time?

The Novice had an answer gift-wrapped for him by the lessons he learned. He assumed another personality, the Persona that expected, and was crafted, to conduct magick. Because the Novice knew that the Persona was only another tool to use in the practice of the Art, it did not simply become a substitute identity for the conscious mind. It was only a tool, although it was an extraordinarily dynamic one.

The primary problem that the Novice faced was learning to use this tool properly, along with the use of meditation, visualization, goal setting, and all the rest of the tools that he had to master. He found a certain degree of difficulty in assuming the Persona, entering the Mind Palace, and imposing his visualizations upon his waking world.

His problems with integrating his tools into himself presented itself as a two-edged sword. He frequently had problems achieving the results that he was seeking, but the tools were so new and unnatural to him that he did not have a problem with the Persona becoming a new egocentric personality.

The Adept has come full circle, and the Persona is now becoming *who he is*. The Adept meditates daily, using visualization to alter the personal history that the Undermind sees, and by this process, giving the Undermind new instructions on what to bring to him. What is more, he has become 'adept' at doing this.

He has come to impose his visualization of his Mind Palace upon the shabby mundane home that he inhabits in the 'real' world, and the Tulpa guardian ardently guards it, since the Adept crafted the Tulpa for that purpose. No one will attempt to rob his home and anyone who considers it will sense a great personal danger, and decide not to intrude. He now sees himself as his Magickal Persona, and therein lies the problem of this level of the Art.

The conscious mind is tenacious, and it will attempt to cloak itself in some identity that will differentiate it as an entity, discrete from the rest of the Universe. The conscious mind *needs* a personality to be what it sees itself as, discrete from the rest of existence. This is a paradox, which must be resolved by the Adept before he can make the transition to the level of Magus.

The Adept has not entirely given up the need for personal power, or identity within the society of which his genetics insist that he should be a part. On a philosophical level, he knows that desires, identity and the insistence of genetics are illusions. They are expediencies or shortcuts to the survival of the Beta or conscious mind, in a task-oriented hunter-gatherer society of the human animal.

There are no clear-cut, logical and simple answers to this paradox. The Adept must *feel* his way to the balance that he seeks. He started this quest for the Art, seeking power from it, and now is starting to realize that power is not important. He now begins to realize that impressing his fellow man with his powers is a useless pursuit. If he heals another or changes the world for any reason, he now knows that he should do so secretly. He has begun to give up power as a purpose in his life.

He also believed that Knowledge must be a reason for practicing the Art. Surely learning all of the wonders of existence is a goal in itself worthy of the efforts. This too has begun to seem a frustrating path, as each question answered leads to another thousand questions.

The stage of the Adept is the journey from the end of the desire for personal power. It is the path through the desire for knowledge, as a goal unto itself. It is the path into the beginning of the world of experiencing, acceptance and the merging of the point of view of the practitioner into the universal mind, which is the source for which the practitioner seeks.

As the Adept struggles with the cascade of new questions that comes to him with each question that he finds answers for, he starts to see a pattern within the questions, which he can also find within the universe around him. He originally found that it is not the goals obtained which bring him satisfaction, but rather the pursuit of those goals, which brings that pleasure.

He found that the goals themselves lose meaning, at the same time that the movement that obtains those goals grows in meaning. He concluded that this is because the power of the Magickal or the quantum world is the important part of the act of obtaining goals, and so he pursued this power relentlessly.

He then discovered that the power too was less important than he originally thought, and so he concluded that the patterns formed within the world, as he sought to complete the Magickal task were the items of importance. He then devoted all of his attention to discovering what these patterns were, in an analysis of the questions of existence, very much related to the scientific methods.

It is when the Adept finally gives up the self-imposed project of analyzing the process of Magick, and its effects upon the world around him, that he begins to make the transition to the stage of the Art that we call the level of the Magus.

7 The Magus

THE MAGUS IS FORGED from the angst and trials of the Adept. He is only possible once the Adept has met his own 'Dark Night of the Soul,' and survived the doubts and confusions. The Adept has struggled with his ego, as it repeatedly attempts to reassert itself, by analyzing the Magickal process, a process that is an attempt by the Practitioner to make the practitioner the Artist, and not part of the Art.

It is when the Adept finally gives up the self-imposed project of analyzing the process of Magick, and its effects upon the world around him, that he begins to make the transition to the stage of the Art that we call the level of the Magus. The Magus has learned the Art of letting go. He releases his need to expect, his need to accept or reject, even his need to be a discrete individual in existence.

He remembers when he was a Novice; he desired personal power above all. He imagined that the world would recognize his value when he swooped into an emergency with his special Magicks and saved the day. Everyone would wipe the sweat from their brows, thankful that a god existed to save them from certain death, or at least, a major inconvenience.

One of the first things that the Magus realizes, when he ascends to that state, is that he no longer has any desire for that recognition from his fellow Man. He would much prefer to work his healings or open the doors of opportunity for his society without once being suspected as the agent of the situation.

The Magus does not avoid the learning of new things; his respect for knowledge is high. Most of what he seeks to understand resides within himself, or within his sensorium. He prefers to seek Wisdom and Experience instead of simple knowledge. There is a flow and a pattern within the lattice of existence that he seeks to comprehend. He can learn more sitting quietly than others can learn in their strenuous quests for the answers.

In many ways, one can draw a parallel, between the ascension in the pursuit of Magick and Money. One can always tell those who are new to having wealth from those who have been rich for many years. One can also tell the inheritors of money from those who created their own wealth.

Those people who recently 'fell into' money act entirely differently from the ones who clawed their way up from nothing to create a legacy. The inheritors throw money around to impress their friends and satisfy their own mercurial impulses, while the Makers spend their money carefully, and even frugally.

Most of the time, the Inheritors will squander their funds in short order, and during the meantime, they will engender envy and greed within those around them until the money is gone. The Makers will be the source of real opportunity for those around them, making every transaction into a win-win for those around them. They will not give their friends money, but they will listen to them, encourage them, and invest in them, after finding a mutually beneficial deal.

If the Inheritors are the money equivalent of the Novice, the Makers are the equivalent of the Adept. What then is the money equivalent of the Magus? That would be the Hidden Millionaire.

The people who create wealth for themselves, and keep it, are a special class of wealthy people. They learned long ago that the best protection against those seeking to take their money is to be a less obvious target. True old wealth does not live lives that are the source of envy. They are comfortable with their lifestyle, always eating well, traveling as they wish, and working on their projects and hobbies industriously. Few of them live idle lifestyles. Most are driven to complete their dreams. Their neighbors seldom know how rich they actually are.

Often the truly wealthy person will be driving an older car, which of course is a hobby to them. They have learned to play the game of money very well, and they recognize that it is indeed a game. It is probably one of the most engrossing games that exist.

The Magus is the Magickal equivalent of the wealthy man I have described. He has learned that there is **no** value to working public miracles. He will often heal the sick or open doors with a Magickal act for a person in need of an opportunity, but he will not advertise the fact. There are times when destiny demands that the Magus does not do these miracles, and for times like these, it is best that he is not known to be able to fix the situation against destiny's mandate.

The Magus reads the patterns that make our world, and he has come to appreciate the experience in all of its forms as both instruction and art. He has come to understand that even pain has its place, and he does not judge his experiences by their convenience any longer.

He wears the Persona that he long ago perfected, but he understands that the Persona is **not him**, merely a **garment** that he wears. As the years go by, he releases his need to cling to his personal identity. He is almost a shadow of his own Undermind, living his days in the dreamlike Satori state, which is the truest form of Mind Unbound.

There is an inherent paradox in the practice of any Magickal Art. It is the ultimate power to change the world around you to conform to your needs and desires, but the thing that it most transforms is the Practitioner. When the Practitioner was an Adept, he quickly became disillusioned with the results of his Art, always unsatisfied with the results of his changes to the world.

As the Practitioner grows in the ability to change things, he begins to feel a bit like the great and imaginary King Ozymandias must have felt, never satisfied with the results of his actions. The Adept stands apart from the world he changes, and this is an implicitly lonely place to stand. The Magus has learned better.

The Magus has been transformed by the Art he plies. He knows that the only Art that means anything must incorporate the Artist as a part of the canvas of the changed universe. He has learned to merge with the world around him, to allow the flows of the universe to wash over him unopposed.

When he has reached the level of Magus, he could exempt himself from aging and illness. He could walk the path between all the worlds that exist. He could, in essence, become a god. He no longer wants any of those things.

The Magus will age and die, just as his neighbors do. He will sicken, and he will have pain. He will be beset by all of the problems that the rest of the world encounters, and he will embrace it all. Any who see him will not consider him odd, other than to note that he has an unusual ability to see the world with humor, and his ability to appreciate everything that happens to and around him.

He loves the experiences that the world brings him. He lives within the world, but he also sees beyond it. He knows that in an infinite number of ways his life and existence is Eternal, and his reach is infinite, and he is content.

The End

If you enjoyed reading this book, please consider leaving a short review where you purchased the book. Reviews are important in getting new Readers to take a chance on reading your book in this bold new world of literature. Every Author needs as many as he can get, and I would be honored if you would review my book.

Magus

About the Author

Magus was born in the midst of a thunderstorm and has enjoyed the comforting sound of rolling thunder ever since. Having inherited a prescient nature, Magus spent his childhood studying history and occult subjects and had a keen interest in the esoteric areas of the physics of relativity and quantum mechanics. Throughout his life, Magus has experienced phenomena that seemed to support the idea of our living in a much more complex and malleable universe than the average person wishes to believe. Over time, he came to believe that most of the events that fill our lives are closely aligned with the laws of quantum mechanics. The years of his life as brought with them the realization that our world is filled with magic and miracles. It is the kind of magic and miracles that comes from the true quantum nature of the world in which we live.

Made in the USA
Middletown, DE
31 January 2020